SEASONAL
OBJECT LESSONS

By

DOROTHY HARRISON PENTECOST

*To my daughters
Jane and Gwendolyn
with love*

MOODY PRESS
CHICAGO

ISBN: 0-8024-7665-1

Tenth Printing, 1975

Printed in the United States of America

CONTENTS

4 *Seasonal Object Lessons*

THANKSGIVING LESSONS

CHRISTMAS LESSONS

MISSIONARY LESSONS

INTRODUCTION

An Object Lesson for Teachers

PREPARATION: Secure an empty cigarette package, an onion, and a bottle of perfume. Place them in a bag to be taken out one at a time.

PRESENTATION

I have three objects in my bag this morning. When you see them, you will wonder how they can teach a spiritual lesson. They are very different in looks but they have one thing in common. They all have an odor.

(Take the cigarette package from the bag.) When my husband rides the commuter train, he always comes home smelling of tobacco smoke. He has to sit by people who are smoking. I asked him, "Where have you been? You smell awful." Of course, I know he has been on the train, and he knows what I mean even though he has gotten used to the smell and doesn't notice it himself. We live in the world and it is hard for us to get away from worldly things. Every time we indulge in worldly things, the children we teach know it, even though we might not realize that it shows.

Worldly things always leave their stamp or flavor on us. We can't fool the children. Though they might not know what to call it, they know that something in our lives doesn't ring true to what we are teaching. We can't fool God either, though sometimes we fool ourselves into believing that our lives are what they should be as Christians.

(Take out the onion.) Here is an onion. I like to put onions into everything possible when I cook. Sometimes I say that I put onions into everything but the ice cream! I especially like onion sandwiches. Occasionally when my husband is away, I eat an onion sandwich. When he comes home, he asks, "What have you been eating?" He knows I have eaten onions. I can't smell my breath but he can. There are many things in our lives that are sinful and repel people from us and away from the Lord Jesus Christ. There are also things that might be all right in themselves but because they might cause others to stumble, they ruin our witness. We don't want to do anything, no matter how innocent, that might cause others to misunderstand our Lord, or lead them to do something wrong because they see what we do. We want everything in our lives to be so sweet and pure and attractive that everyone who comes in contact with us will want to know Christ as their Saviour too.

(Take the perfume from the bag.) Here is a bottle of perfume. Do you know some ladies who wear nice perfume? I do, and I like to be near them because they smell so lovely. I have a little niece who likes to sample my perfumes, and even though we tell her not to, she still puts some on. When she comes into the kitchen, her mother and I know what she has done. We can smell it in the air, but she can't. She is always so surprised that we know she used it. A real Christian should be like that to be pleasing to the Lord. We should have the sweetness of the Lord in us all the time that attracts others to our Saviour. We can only get that sweetness and drawing power by spending much time in the presence of the Lord in prayer and in meditation on His Word. God told Moses to make a perfume to be used only in the Tabernacle (Exod. 30:34-38). He also said that no one else was to use this perfume. In this way, the priests who went into the Tabernacle to minister would be surrounded with this special perfume. When they came out again, all the people around them would know that they had been in the presence of the Lord because they could smell the perfume. Our lives are to be a sweet savor or a fragrance of Christ to all the people around us (II Cor. 2:14-16). They should know the minute we enter the room that we have been with the Lord. There should be something very different about our lives that shows people that we have been living with the Lord. This isn't something that we can manifest in our own lives. It can only be given by the Holy Spirit as we keep our lives free from sin so He can do His full work in us.

The boys and girls you are teaching are getting some kind of fragrance from your life. No matter how much Bible you are teaching them, you are also teaching them by your life. Before God ask these questions: Which place am I? Am I indulging in worldly things that keep God from working through me? Am I the kind of Christian who wants my own way so much that I'll do things I know will repel others and hurt my testimony? Or, am I sure that I am the kind of Christian who is living so close to the Lord that the very sweetness and fragrance of the Lord is attracting people to Christ? Let the Lord bring the necessary conviction in your life. Pray for a closer walk with Him. Nothing would please Him more than a real determination on your part to be "a sweet savor of Christ" to all around you.

NEW YEAR'S LESSONS

NEW YEAR'S RESOLUTIONS

PREPARATION: Write down some New Year's resolutions which might be similar to those which children would make.

PRESENTATION

Did you make any New Year's resolutions this week? I have written some down on a paper I brought with me this morning. Let me read a few of them to you. "I will read my Bible and pray everyday. I will study my lessons so I will get good grades in school. I will help my mother. I will obey my parents. I will not fight with my brothers and sisters." (Let the children add to this list any that they have made.) What happened to the resolutions you made last year and the year before that? Oh, you weren't able to keep them? Perhaps you forgot all about them in a few weeks or a month. If you had been able to keep them, you wouldn't have needed to make any new ones, would you?

We have failed to keep our New Year's resolutions for two reasons. First, because we really didn't want to keep them, and second, because we tried to keep them in our own strength. Oh, you say, you are mistaken! You did want to keep them. Let's think back for a few minutes over this past year. Why didn't you read your Bible and pray everyday? Was it because you wanted to sleep later in the morning, or you wanted to watch a favorite television program? Did you disobey your parents because you wanted to have your own way? Was it a desire to play with your friends that kept you from studying enough to get good grades in school? Didn't you fight and quarrel with your brothers and sisters because they were keeping you from having the things you wanted? If we are really honest about it, we failed to keep our resolutions because we are self-centered and wanted to have our own way more than to do the things that we know are pleasing to God.

But suppose that you did try very hard over and over to keep these resolutions and still you failed. Perhaps you failed because you were trying to keep them in your own strength instead of letting Christ do it for you.

There is one very important verse in the Bible that will be a help to us as we start this new year. It would be a good thing for each of

us to memorize it, so we can say it over in our
hearts every time we are tempted to please ourselves instead of the Lord. (Read Gal. 2:20.)
It says that we are *dead*. It means that everyone of us who belongs to Christ should remember that God sees us as if we were crucified
when Christ was and that from now on we are
to treat ourselves as though we were dead. We
are not to have our own way any more. Even
though we are still alive in our bodies and go
about on this earth, we should live as though
we were dead to our own wishes, our desires,
and having our own way. It is not we who are
to be pleased any more, and it is not we who are
to try to live a Christian life. Christ is now living in us. He is the Head of our lives and we
are to let Him live out His life through us. We
are to let Christ live the kind of life He wants,
and that kind of life will often be very different
from the selfish kind of life that we have been
living before. By faith, or by believing, we are
to accept the fact that our self life is dead and
that Christ living in us will lead and guide us
into the kind of life He wants us to live. It is
only as we let Christ live out His life through
us, that we can live this new kind of life. We
have tried and tried and failed and failed every
time we have tried to live like Christ in our own

strength. Just as you received Christ as your Saviour by believing that He died on the cross for you, so you are to believe that Christ will live His life through you as you let Him. Just believe what God says in this verse.

Right now, let's bow our heads and ask the Lord Jesus Christ to help us remember that we are to live as though we were dead, and ask Him to live through us a life that pleases Him.

CHRIST OUR PATTERN

PREPARATION: Secure a dress pattern

PRESENTATION

Does your mother make any of your clothes?
Does she ever make her own dresses? Even if
she doesn't, I am sure that you have seen a
pattern like the one I brought with me this
morning.

I made a dress for myself by this pattern. I
carefully took all the pieces of the pattern out
of the envelope like this. (Take out a few
pieces.) Then I fitted them on the material,
pinned them together and cut out the dress.
After I sewed all the pieces of material together, I had a dress that looked just like the picture
on the front of the envelope. No matter how
many times I use this pattern, it will always be
a dress that looks like this. It will never be a
suit, a coat, or a pair of pajamas.

I could never make a dress if I just took the
scissors and cut any place on the material. One
day my baby daughter did and all the material
that she cut was ruined. I couldn't make any-

thing out of what was left. There are people
who think they can live a Christian life without Christ and without following His example.
They think that their way of living will get
them to Heaven just as surely as taking the
Lord Jesus Christ as their Saviour. Listen
while I read you a verse from Proverbs 16:25.
God says that their ways aren't right and it will
lead only to death. When we try to live the way
we think is right, it is always wrong because
God says that we don't know how to live a
Christian life. We will make a mess of our lives
just as cutting material without a pattern will
ruin it.

There is only one true pattern that we can
follow to live a Christian life, and that is the
Lord Jesus Christ. The most important thing
Christ did for us was to die on the cross for
our sins so that believing in Him we might be
saved. Even after we are saved we still can't
live the Christian life without following Christ.
In many places in the Bible, we are told that He
is our example or pattern for living (I Tim.
1:16). We are to walk the same way He walked.
"Christ also suffered for us, leaving us an example, that ye should follow his steps" (I Peter
2:21b).

Since Christ is the only One we can follow to

be sure we are living a Christian life, where can we find out just what Christ is like? Yes, the Bible is the only place we can trust to tell us what Christ did and said and how He lived. Sometimes, God uses our teachers and ministers to help us understand the things written in the Word, but it must all come from God's Word to be sure that it is true. When we faithfully follow what is written in the Bible, we know that our lives will be Christ-like. Just as we know if we follow this pattern, a dress like the one in the picture will always be the result. If our lives are a mess or not Christ-like, we can be sure that we are following our own ways and not following Christ. When we follow Christ, we will always be pleasing to Him and our lives will be like His.

As we start into this New Year, you must decide whom you are going to follow. Will it be your own way or Christ's way? Let us determine in our hearts that this year we will follow Christ, no matter what it costs us so that our lives will be Christ-like.

NEW YEAR'S EVE

PREPARATION: Let a large clock run down, set it at 12, and take it with you without starting it. A clock that ticks loudly is best.

PRESENTATION

People in our country and in many others celebrate the coming of a new year. Lots of people have parties to see the new year in, and others go downtown in large cities to gather in a crowd to cheer for the new year. In Philadelphia there is a large clock on the William Penn statue that is lighted at night so it can be seen for miles around. On New Year's Eve many thousands of people gather around the court house to celebrate the new year and to see the clock when it is exactly midnight. Five minutes before midnight, the lights on the clock are turned off and everyone watches carefully, because at the stroke of midnight, the lights in the clock and around the court house are turned on and all the people cheer and make all kinds of noises. Has your mother ever let you stay up on New Year's Eve to see the new year come

18

in at midnight? What did you do to celebrate?

I have brought a large clock with me, which is set at midnight to make us think of the new year. When we see a clock, I am sure we all think about time. We look at the clock to see when we have to get up in the morning, when we have to go to school, when we have to go to a music lesson, etc. We are all controlled most of the time by a clock. There is a time set for church and Sunday school so that we will all get there together and can have a service. There is a time for our meals, and a time to go to bed. When David was speaking to the Lord through a verse in the Book of Psalms, he said, "My times are in thy hands." This is true of each one of us. God is the One who decides just what is going to happen to us in the new year. The time to be born, the time to die, the times of happiness and health, and even the times of trial are all in God's hands.

I am going to start this clock now by winding it (or plugging it in an electric socket). We will pretend that the new year is starting right now. We have a year ahead of us. We have twelve months. We have 52 weeks, and we have 365 days. God has given each of us the same amount of time. No matter how young or old, how poor or rich, how big or little we are, or in what state or country we live, we all have the same amount of time.

Have you thought about what you want to do with the time that God has given you in this new year? Have you decided whether you are going to use it for yourself or for God? In Ephesians 5:16, we have a verse that is just perfect for us to use for this new year. "Redeeming the time, because the days are evil." "To redeem" means to "buy up" or to "make the best use of our time," because there is evil all around us. The verse before this tells us how we are to walk as Christians, so I believe that God wants us to be careful to use our time living a life that is pleasing to Him. The verse right after this one tells us that we are to understand and do the will of God. What two better ways can we find to use our time this new year than to walk in a way that is pleasing to God and in doing His will? This is really just two ways of saying the same thing, for when we are doing God's will we are living a life that is pleasing to Him.

When you hear about the new year, or look at the clock, think of what God's Word says about "redeeming the time," and be determined to make all your time count for the Lord Jesus Christ this year.

FEAR NOT

PREPARATION: Take a light to make some shadows with your hands.

PRESENTATION

(Make some shadows on the wall with your hands or some objects that you have taken with you.) I know some little boys and girls who are afraid of shadows. That is foolish, isn't it? Shadows can't hurt anyone. Have you had fun making shadows when you were out in the sun? Even if your shadow jumps up and down on someone else, it still couldn't hurt, could it? Shadows are just a reflection. Have you ever been afraid at night of something that you later found out was just a shadow?

People who know about such things tell us that 85 per cent of the things that we fear never come to pass. Over and over God's Word tells us, "fear not," and not to be afraid. Often we make ourselves miserable and unhappy and sometimes even sick over something that isn't real, like the shadows. David said: "Yea, though I walk through the valley of the shadow of death, I will fear no evil: for thou art with me" (Ps. 23:4). Our fear is real and it makes us uncomfortable, but we must put everything in our lives in God's hands, whether real or like the shadows. Do you know that we are told 365 times to "fear not," or words that mean the same thing in the Bible? Maybe that is God's way of emphasizing the fact that we are not to be afraid any day during the new year. He knows that there are things that will make us afraid so He has given us many verses to help us. (Read Ps. 56:3, 4.) This is a good verse for us to learn so we can use it through the coming year.

Even when Christ was here on earth with the disciples, they were sometimes afraid. Once when there was a bad storm while they were in a boat, they were so afraid that they awakened Jesus and asked Him to save them. He asked them, "Why are ye so fearful? Oh, ye of little faith." He meant that if they had completely trusted Him, they wouldn't have been afraid. Later, when He told them that He was going back to Heaven, they were afraid again, and He said, "Let not your heart be troubled, neither let it be afraid" (John 14:27). He promised that His peace would be with them so they wouldn't be afraid.

As we start this new year, we want to talk about how we can keep from being afraid. Knowing and trusting the Lord Jesus Christ is the only way we can keep from being afraid. How can we know Him better? Yes, we have two ways of knowing Jesus Christ and living closer to Him. We have our Bibles to read and learn more about Him and what He has promised to do for us. And we also have the right to talk to Him in prayer and have His promise that He will answer.

God has a plan for each one of us and He has made the promise that if we belong to the Lord Jesus Christ everything that happens to us is "working together for good" (Rom. 8:28). God sends only those things into our lives that He knows will be for our good. God is taking complete care of each of us so there is nothing to fear. Just ask God to help you trust Him more and not to be afraid. He will gladly help you.

All of us who have taken the Lord Jesus Christ as our Saviour need never be afraid of death, because God has promised that when we leave this earth we will go to be with Him. But if any of you have not taken Christ as your Saviour, now would be the best time (II Cor. 6:2). What better time would there be to take Christ as Saviour than the first day of this new

year? Now you can start this year without any
fear, knowing that God will work out everything in your life.

CONFESSION

PREPARATION: Make two large hearts the same size out of white paper or cardboard. Take a black crayon, an eraser, and a red cloth large enough to cover the hearts. When the lesson starts have one heart hidden under the red cloth on the table.

PRESENTATION

As the old year is dying out and the new year is starting, we hear a lot of talk about the mistakes and failures of the past year. Many people plan to do better in the new year by making resolutions, but for some reason they always come to the end of the year with hearts full of sin.

I have a white heart here in my hand to stand for all the boys and girls who have taken the Lord Jesus Christ as Saviour, and have had all their sins washed away. Those sins are gone forever, and we can never be judged for them any more because Christ paid the price that was required of us. (Read Rom. 6:23.)

We all wish that once we have asked Christ

to come into our hearts that we couldn't sin any more. But unhappily that is not true. We still have the old sin nature in us that makes us sin, and often we want to sin and enjoy that sin even though we know that we are displeasing God. Satan wants us to sin too, so he uses the old desires in our hearts to make us fall into temptation and sin.

On this heart we will write some of the sins that we usually commit and see if we can wash those sins away. Will you name a sin that you think boys and girls are apt to do? Yes, I believe that lying is a real temptation, because we think we can often escape punishment by lying about it. I have an eraser in my hand that we are going to let represent all the good things that we might think would help us get rid of that sin. (Let the children who name the sins come up and try to erase them.) We will let the eraser represent joining the church. You see, that joining the church doesn't make that sin go away. Name another sin. Cheating is one that is often hard for boys and girls to avoid when it is so easy to copy someone else's paper. We will let the eraser represent attending Sunday school, and we will see if it will take away this sin. It doesn't work, does it? Someone may name another sin. Not reading your Bible and praying is one, for it seems so hard for boys and girls to find time in their busy lives to read and pray. We will let the eraser represent giving money to missionaries and you may see if that will take away the sin on the heart. We have time to speak of one more sin. Being disobedient to our parents is something that I am sure all of you have trouble with. We will let the eraser represent being good and kind to others. You may see if it will erase that sin. (If someone tears the heart with the eraser, impress upon the children that the heart which is full of sin is the broken heart that is heavy and unhappy with the load of guilt.)

The only way to find out what we are to do as Christians about the sins that enter our hearts is to look into God's Word. God has the answer for every need, and He has a very plain answer for this one. (Read I John 1:9.) We must confess each sin. That means telling God just what we did and being truly sorry for it. He is faithful to keep His promise and forgive because Christ has already paid for that sin. (Pick up clean heart and red cloth and hold both in front of the sin-filled heart.) We are going to put this red napkin over this sin-filled heart because "the blood of Jesus Christ his Son cleanseth us from all sin," and that means the sins that we commit after we are saved, as well as the ones before we are saved. Now, as I remove the red napkin, look at this restored and clean heart. God will do that for everyone of us when we confess our sins. The minute you realize that you have done something wrong, confess it to God and keep your heart free from sin and your life in fellowship with the Lord.

VALENTINE LESSONS

VALENTINE BOX

PREPARATION: Secure a white box for a Valentine box (the deeper the lid the better). Decorate the top with red hearts in the shape of a cross. Make a slit in the top large enough to slip the paper hearts through. Put a false top under the box lid to hold the black hearts that are put through the cross. Make three black hearts and three white hearts. Put the white hearts inside the box before the lesson begins.

PRESENTATION

I suppose that all of you have a Valentine box at school. I have made one for our class to use this morning. Look at the front. I am sure this box is decorated differently than any you have at school. There is a cross on our box.

Valentine's Day is supposed to be a day of expressing our love for one another. This cross was put here to remind us that the greatest love of all was expressed on the cross of Calvary. This shows God's love for the world that made Him give His Son for our salvation. It shows

31

Christ's love for us in giving up all His heavenly glory to take the sins of the world on Himself and to die that we might live through Him.

Here are a few sin-filled hearts to represent boys and girls without Christ in their hearts. God says that our hearts are "deceitful above all things, and desperately wicked" (Jer. 17:9). "There is none righteous, no, not one" (Rom. 3:10). "All have sinned and come short of the glory of God" (Rom. 3:23).

I have put the cross on the front of this box to show us that "Christ died for our sins" (I Cor. 15:3, 4). He took your sins and mine and the sins of everyone in the world and died for those sins. Now, anyone who wants to be saved has only to ask the Lord Jesus Christ to save him. This cross is made of red paper to remind us of the blood of Christ that He shed to wash our sins away (I John 1:7).

Three of you may help me now. Each of you may take one of these sinful hearts and bring it to the cross of Christ. Just push it through the little slot I have made in the top. Now, let's open the box and see what has happened to these hearts. Take them out and show them to the other boys and girls. They are white now! All of their sins have been washed away. God has promised that if we ask the Lord Jesus

Christ to come into our hearts to save us, He will come and He will always stay in our hearts.

If anyone of you has never asked the Lord Jesus Christ to save you, you can do it right now. Just bow your head and say in your heart, "Dear Jesus, I believe You died for me. Please come into my heart and save me. Thank You. Amen." That is all you need to do because Christ has done all the rest that God requires. If you asked Him to come into your heart and you really meant what you said, you have had your sins washed away and Christ is living in your heart right now.

HEARTS

PREPARATION : Buy four small Valentine boxes. Glue a piece of black paper across the top of the bottom of the first. Put some small stones in the second; some thorns or weeds in the third; and some good soil in the fourth. Take a package of seed and print THE WORD across it.

PRESENTATION

Valentine's Day has often been called Heart's Day also. The Bible has so much to say about hearts and about love that we could almost call it a Valentine Book. God must be very interested in our hearts because there are so many verses that tell about the wrong kind of hearts, and many more that tell of the kind of hearts that God wants us to have. We are told that some hearts are set to do evil, are desperately wicked, are far from God, hardened, rebellious, blind and unbelieving. God says that the heart that is pleasing to Him is the heart that is clean, pure, obedient, honest, wholly devoted to God, and is fixed on God.

I have brought four Valentine heart-shaped boxes to show us how the Word of God affects different kinds of hearts of people. Christ told a parable-story of the sower and the seed. Then He explained that the seed was the Word of God, or the Bible. He said that the different kinds of soil in which the seed was planted are like the hearts of people who hear God's Word. I have also brought a package of seed and I have printed, "THE WORD OF GOD" on it so you will remember what it stands for.

Now, let's open these hearts one at a time and plant some of the seed and see what happens. This first heart hears the Word but won't let it come into his heart. This person has heard that Christ died on the cross to save him from his sin, but he won't take Christ as his Saviour. This heart is full of sin. See, the seed rolls off the top of the heart. Let's open the second heart and put some seed in this one. This heart receives Christ as Saviour. See, the heart is white inside to remind us that her sins have been washed away. But, look at the heart! It is full of something else. How can seed grow in those rocks and bring forth any fruit? It can't. Christ says that the stones keep the seed from growing, and when the sun comes up it will wither and be so dried up it can't be much good.

Now, let's look at the third box. This person is saved when he hears the Word because this heart has had all the sins washed away too. But, look, this heart has something in it too! It is full of thorns. How can the seed grow very well in all that mass of thorns? Christ says that after some of us have taken Him as Saviour, we get so busy with the things that we have to do and with getting more money and more things that we don't have time for reading the Bible and praying, and going to church services and places where we can study the Word. A life like that can't bear much fruit for God; it is too full of other things.

Now, let's look into this last box. It is full of good soil that is just right for receiving the seed of the Word. This person has taken Christ as Saviour and Lord, and his life is now ready to bear much fruit for the Lord Jesus Christ. This is the kind of heart that He wants each of us to have (Matt. 13:3-8, 18-23).

I can't look down into your heart. Only you and God know what kind of heart you have. I hope that none of you has a black heart like this first one. But if you do, right now you can take Christ as your Saviour, by asking Him to come into your heart. I hope that each of us will be

careful to keep our hearts clean before God so
that we can bring forth much fruit to His glory.
(Also see John 15:1-14.)

ALL OF ME

PREPARATION: Make a large double heart to open on the side like a book. Decorate with lace around the edge, or with paper doilies. Print ALL OF ME across the front, and put a picture of yourself inside. If you don't have a picture use one from a magazine to represent you.

PRESENTATION

I have made a valentine to give to someone. After we have talked awhile, I am going to tell you whom this valentine is for. Have you taken time to carefully read all the verses on your valentines? Sometimes, you get so many that all you do is look at the names of the ones who sent them to you. Many of the verses say, "I give all of myself to you," or "I want to be yours alone," or other words like that. You will notice that I have printed ALL OF ME on the front of my valentine, because I really and truly want to give all of me to the one this valentine was made for.

God says that He wants all of each one of us.

(Read Rom. 12:1, 2.) These verses say that
because of what the Lord Jesus Christ has done
for us in dying on the cross, we are asked to
give ourselves completely to God as a living
sacrifice. We are not asked to die for Christ
but we are asked to live for Him. But living for
Christ is a sacrifice as much as dying for Him.
It means that everyday we are to forget or give
up our desires and wishes and do only those
things that are pleasing to God. The next verse
tells us that we are not to be like the children
who don't know Christ as their Saviour but we
are to be different. We are to do God's will for
us, not because we have to or because we can't
help it, but because we love Him so much that
we want to do the things that please Him. God
says that He has a good, perfect and acceptable
will for each one of us, and if we are willing to
do what He has planned for us He will tell us
what His will is (John 7:17). He doesn't show
us His will first and let us make a choice between our will and His. We must first make
up our minds to do God's will and then He will
tell us what it is.

Now I will open the valentine and show you
what is inside. It is a picture of myself, and
this valentine is for the Lord. I want to show
my love for Him, and my appreciation for what

Christ has done for me in saving me, by giving all of myself back to Him. I want to do His will all the rest of my life.

Perhaps God is talking to your heart. Maybe you have been living to suit yourself with little or no thought of what God wants you to do. If you feel that you want to give yourself completely to God to be used by Him in any way that He wants, why don't you bow your head right now and tell Him? You will bring honor and glory to God when you willingly give up your right to yourself and gladly give all of you to be used in any way God wants to use you.

POINTED HEARTS

PREPARATION: Make a large paper heart. Print
DELIGHT THYSELF ALSO IN across the top.
Draw a short arrow from these words to the
middle of the heart. Under the arrow, cut a
square hole big enough to show one word at a
time from the circle underneath. Make a
paper circle to go behind the heart with the
following words printed on it, PLAY, TV,
MONEY, HOME, THINGS, and THE LORD. Space
these so they will show through the hole in
the heart one at a time. Connect the heart
and circle with a brad, so the circle will ro-
tate behind the heart.

PRESENTATION

I brought a valentine with me this morning
with part of a Bible verse on it (Ps. 37:4). It
says that we are to delight ourselves in something; there is just a hole below the arrow. "To
delight" means to take pleasure in, or to be
happy with something.

We want to talk today about pointed hearts.
Now you know our hearts aren't pointed, are

41

they? I am sure you have seen pictures in a book or studied in school what our hearts look like. When God talks about our hearts, He doesn't mean just the physical organ that pumps the blood through our bodies. He means the part of us that loves, that wants things, that thinks, and decides what we will do.

What does your heart like most or delight in the most? Which way is your heart pointed? (Turn circle to show PLAY.) Is it play that gives you the most pleasure? (Turn circle to TV.) Or does watching the television give the most pleasure? (Turn circle to THINGS.) Do you find your most delight in having a lot of things like clothes, toys and pets, etc.? (Turn circle to MONEY.) Is money something that you want more than anything else? Do you feel if you had all the money you wanted, so you could buy everything you wanted, that you would be perfectly happy and satisfied? (Turn circle to HOME.) Do you take the most delight in your home and parents? As wonderful as they are, and as thankful as we should be for these things, that is still not what we should take our most delight in. (Turn circle to THE LORD.) Our verse says that we should take delight or find our greatest pleasure in the Lord. We should put the Lord first in our lives. Our greatest joy should be in the fact that we know the only living and true God, and that we have the Lord Jesus Christ as our Saviour.

We should find our joy in the Lord because He made us and then sent Christ to save us. We should also delight ourselves in the Lord because it pleases and glorifies God for us to do it. But God has added a wonderful promise to this verse. He has promised that all who find their delight in the Lord will have the desires of their hearts. That sounds too good to be true, but God always does what He promises! Maybe some of you are thinking that it would be impossible for God to make a promise like that because we might want something that isn't right for us to have. If we are truly putting our delight in the Lord first of all, I can assure you that we will only want the things that are pleasing to Him. Then, when the things are pleasing to Him, it is easy for Him to grant our every wish.

Which way is your heart pointed, to the Lord or to your self? Is your heart pointed to all the pleasures of play, TV, and money, or is it pointed to the Lord? You are the only one who knows the condition of your heart. I can't tell what is in your heart. Your best friend can't tell either. What does God see when He looks

at your heart? If you know that your heart has
been wrong, won't you tell God that now and
ask Him to forgive you and give you a real desire to put Him first in your life?

LOVE

PREPARATION: There is nothing to take for this lesson.

PRESENTATION

I couldn't bring an object for our lesson this morning, but I know that every one of you knows about the thing that I am going to talk about. I want to talk about love. Have you seen a boy and a girl who are in love with each other? I know you have because I have seen you snicker and make fun of the way they act. You think it is funny now, but when you get a little older you will understand.

When people are in love they want to be with the one they love all the time. They aren't happy when they have to be separated, and when they must be separated they are thinking about each other most of the time. Another thing, you will notice, is that people who are in love aren't interested in pleasing themselves any more. They just want to do everything the one they love wants to do. They don't want to spend any money on themselves. They just want to save it so they can give nice gifts to the one they love. People in love want to hear all they can about the one they love and like to talk about each other. They tell each other secrets that they don't want anyone else to know. Just as soon as a young man falls in love with a girl something happens to the way he lives. He stops going with other girls; he just wants to be with the one he loves. Sometimes if you are close enough you might hear him say, "I love you with all my heart."

God wants us to love Him in the same way. His Word tells us about the kind of love that He wants from all of us, whether we are young or old. Let me read Matthew 22:37. God wants us to love Him with all our hearts, our souls, and our minds. That means He wants us to love Him with all of us, doesn't it? If we really love God in that way, do you think it would make a difference in the way we live? It should make a big difference. Now, it should be our desire to be with the Lord constantly in prayer and in the reading of His Word to learn more about Him. It should make us want to refuse to do the things that we know will displease Him, and make us very anxious to find and do the things that will honor and glorify Him. When we are really in love with the Lord, we

will want to use our money for the things that
He likes. We will be very careful to contribute
to the work of the church and to the work of
missionaries, and to those who need aid in witnessing to the Lord in any way, rather than
spending the money on ourselves. There will
be things we will talk to the Lord about that we
will never mention to anyone else, even the
dearest person to us on the earth. He will be so
precious to us that our thoughts and actions
will always please Him. We will be happy and
proud to tell others that we belong to the Lord
and show them how they can take Christ as
their Saviour too.

Even though God has millions and millions of
Christians who love Him, He wants each one of
us to love Him too. "For God so loved the world,
that he gave his only begotten Son, that who-
soever believeth in him should not perish, but
have everlasting life." "Christ loved us and
gave himself for us." Both God the Father, and
God the Son showed their love by making a way
for us to be saved. They did it because they love
us and they want our love in return. Have you
ever said deep down in your heart to God, "I
love You with all my heart, soul and mind," and
really meant it? That makes God so happy that
I hope you will do it more. Don't do it because

God's Word tells us to, but because we really want to and we really mean what we say. You can learn to love God more by talking to Him in prayer and by reading the Bible often. As you find out how much He has done and is doing for you, you can't help but love Him with all your heart.

EASTER LESSONS

A MOMENT

PREPARATION: Secure a stop watch. If this is not possible, the lesson can be taught with the winking of the eye.

PRESENTATION

This is a stop watch. It is something like the watches we wear on our wrists. It is a small, portable timepiece. Our watches run all the time. This watch only runs when I push my finger down on the lever on top. It marks off time only as long as I keep my finger on it. When I release it, the timing stops. It is often used to check athletes to see how long they can run or fight, etc. I brought it with me this morning to show how long one moment of time is. Would any of you like to guess how long it is? I will time you with the watch. (Time several.) Now I want you all to be very still while I time exactly one moment for you.

God's Word tells us that the most amazing, spectacular miracle is going to happen in one moment of time. We just learned that isn't very long, is it? Listen while I read you some verses.

(Read I Cor. 15:51, 52. Use the word "secret" in place of "mystery.") Now wink your eye. How long did that take? It didn't take as long as the moment we just timed. What is this wonderful secret that God says is going to happen in a moment or in the twinkling of an eye? He promises that our bodies are going to be changed from earthly bodies to new wonderful spiritual bodies that will be fitted for Heaven. A trumpet is going to sound and Christ will appear in the air, and all Christians will immediately have their corrupt bodies changed to heavenly bodies.

All through this same chapter, Paul tells us that when we rise from the dead at Christ's return, our earthly bodies will be heavenly bodies, our natural bodies that are weak and often sick will be spiritual bodies raised in power, well and strong. There won't be any more sickness or pain. Those who have suffered physically here on earth will suffer no more. People with deformed and ugly bodies will be made straight and beautiful. All of us will be made strong and well again. These bodies will never die and we will live with the Lord forever (Rev. 21:4).

Does all this sound too hard to believe? God made our bodies the first time, so it will be very easy for Him to remake them in a moment's time. He made man in His own image and likeness, but sin ruined man and brought spiritual death. Adam and Eve were the first people who ever lived, and for a while they lived without sinning. Then one day they disobeyed God by eating the fruit from the one tree that God had told them they must not. Right then sin entered into their hearts, and since that time sin has been in the hearts of everyone who has ever lived. Because of sin, our bodies get sick, suffer pain and finally die physically. If Adam and Eve had never sinned, they would have lived forever in the Garden of Eden. When sin entered the earth, so did death. God planned a way for us to escape from spiritual death, and a way for us to have our bodies made new. By believing in the death and the resurrection of the Lord Jesus Christ, we can have this new life, and a new, glorified body, and never die again.

VICTORY

PREPARATION: Take several clippings about some kind of victory from the newspaper and, if possible, a Victory medal or ribbon such as was worn by soldiers during the last World War.

PRESENTATION

I have some newspaper clippings with me this morning that I want to read to you. This headline says, "Oklahoma Wins Victory in Cotton Bowl." Maybe you saw the game on the TV. Do you know what it means to have a victory? I know you do for I have heard you talk about having victories in your school ball games. It means to win or to triumph over something or someone. Here is another story of a mother who was very ill with polio and now is able to take care of her family while sitting in a wheel chair. I have a very old paper here that was printed the day the second World War ended. It tells about the U.S. victory over Japan and Germany. Some of our servicemen still have Victory medals and ribbons to wear on their uniforms to show that they fought with an army that had won battles over the enemy.

Easter should be a great day of thanksgiving and rejoicing because the resurrection of the Lord Jesus Christ means that we can have victory over death just as He did. Most people fear death more than anything else that can happen to them. Why are people so afraid to die? I believe it is because they don't know what the life after death is like or where they are going. Most of them know that their lives have been sinful and they don't deserve to go to Heaven. How can we conquer a fear of death? God's Word has the answer for us. (Read Heb. 2:14, 15.) This verse is talking about the Lord Jesus Christ. He took the form of a man and was born as a baby. Then when He was grown, He went to the cross, taking the sins of everyone in the world—past, present, future. By His death and resurrection, He destroyed the power that Satan had over death. In this way, everyone who takes the Lord Jesus Christ as Saviour is delivered from a fear of death because we know that Christ has taken our place, and His death frees us from spiritual death or separation from God.

Have you seen this victory sign made with the first two fingers? Perhaps you have seen

it at a ball game. Someone started this little
sign of victory during the second World War,
and it is still being used. As Christians, we
can use a victory sign too because we have
victory over death. It is not our victory, and
nothing we can do will give us victory. Our
victory comes only through the Lord Jesus
Christ. (Read I Cor. 15:55-57.) Our victory
is over death and its sting. Sin is the sting of
death because sin keeps us from Heaven and
God's presence. Christ has overcome sin by
His death on the cross, carrying our sins and
paying the price that God demands. Death cannot have a sting or fear for us if we are sure
that we are in Christ Jesus. He has gone before
us and made the way for us to come to Him
when we leave this earth. Our bodies die and
are laid in the grave, but our souls and spirits
go immediately to be with the Lord. When
Christ comes for all who belong to Him, our
bodies will be changed into wonderful new
bodies that will never die again. Our souls and
spirits will be united to our bodies and we will
spend all eternity with the Lord.

Verse 57 says, that knowing what Christ has
done for us should fill our hearts with thanksgiving instead of the fear we used to know.
If you have taken the Lord Jesus Christ as your

Saviour, this Easter should be a wonderful day for you as you realize what Christ has done for you. This should be another special Thanksgiving day for you. But if you have never taken Christ as your Saviour, Easter is a day of warning to you because Christ has been raised from the dead and He has promised to all who believe on Him that He will raise them from the dead too. Right now, if you have never asked Christ to come into your heart, just ask Him. He will gladly come in and never leave you.

MADE NEW IN CHRIST

PREPARATION: Wear some new clothes or take something else that is new. Flowers can also be used.

PRESENTATION

You boys and girls are wearing so many new clothes this morning that sometimes I didn't recognize you until I could see your faces. I have something new on this morning too. (Name what it is.) I also have a lily here that is so new it just opened up this morning. Easter is a time of thinking of new things. There are new leaves growing on the trees; new flowers just blooming; new birds have returned from the south; and new grass is beginning to show on all the lawns. We all like new things, I am sure. You want new toys, new friends, and the grown folks like new homes and new cars, etc. Sometimes getting new things costs so much that many of us can't afford to have them.

This Easter should make us very happy because we can all have the two most wonderful new things in all the world without any money.

Anyone can have these things because God and the Lord Jesus Christ paid all the necessary price for us. We can have a new life through the Lord Jesus Christ because He died on the cross for us. God said that "the wages of sin is death." Someone had to die for those sins, and Christ loved us so much that He took your sins and mine on the cross when He died. Now when we ask the Lord Jesus Christ to save us, we automatically have a wonderful new eternal life given us and we can never be separated from God again. This new life makes us fitted for Heaven. It makes us God's dear children in a very special way, and it gives us His promise that He will take care of every need that we can have.

We have this wonderful assurance that we are going to be given new bodies because the Lord Jesus Christ rose from the dead. Everyone who belongs to Christ is going to be resurrected when He comes back again, and given new bodies. If we are still living when He comes again, we will be given our new bodies without having to die. But whether we are dead or alive when He comes again, all who belong to the Lord Jesus Christ will go to Heaven to be forever with the Lord.

I have heard boys and girls say that they

would like to know just what their new bodies
will look like. Sometime read I Corinthians 15,
or have someone read it to you and explain it.
That chapter tells us a lot about our new bodies.
We can tell some things about our new bodies
because after Christ rose from the dead 500
people saw Him, and some of the Gospel writers
have told us what He was like. Remember, He
could eat because He ate breakfast with the disciples on the morning after they went fishing.
He passed through closed doors without open-
ing them. The disciples recognized Him so His
body must have looked something like the one
He first had. He had a new glorified body that
was fitted for living in Heaven. He rose in the
air as He went back into Heaven.

I think the most wonderful promise in all the
Bible for Christians is I John 3:2. Listen, while
I read it. It says that we can't understand now
just what our new bodies are going to be like,
but we are promised that we will be like the
Lord Jesus Christ. That is all we need to know,
isn't it? We will see Him and be with Him and
be like Him. We can't realize how glorious that
is going to be. Just believe it and thank God
for what He has done for us. (Also see Phil.
3:21.)

ASLEEP IN CHRIST

PREPARATION : Secure a small doll bed and a
doll that closes its eyes.

PRESENTATION

We are going to talk about sleeping this
morning, so I brought this doll bed and a doll
that closes her eyes when she is laid down. We
will put the doll in the bed and pretend that she
has gone to sleep. All of you have to go to bed
at night and sleep. Maybe you don't want to
go when your mother insists that you do, but
you go. After awhile, you would get so tired
that you would want to go to sleep anyway.

When Christ was here on earth, he talked
about a Christian's death as being sleep. Christ
never said that a person was dead, but He called
it being asleep. When Lazarus had died and his
family had sent word to the Lord Jesus Christ
to come, He told the disciples, "Our friend
Lazarus sleepeth" (John 11:11). The disciples
didn't understand that He meant that Lazarus
was really dead until Christ told them plainly
that he was dead.

61

Christ wants us to think of death as just going to sleep and waking up in Heaven with Him. You know how you get ready for bed when you are tired, perhaps your mother tucks you in, and kisses you good night. You go to sleep, and when you wake up it is morning and you are rested and ready for another day. When our bodies become old, tired and ill, we go to sleep in Christ and just wake up seeing Christ, and we start a wonderful new life in Heaven. It should not be a time of fear or dread when we die, but a time of joy and happiness to know that we will be forever with the Lord. Just think of your mother tucking you in bed and then waking up to see the Lord Jesus Christ!

When Paul was writing a letter to the people in a church at Thessalonica, he referred to the Christian who is dead as being asleep too. God told us through Paul that He didn't want us to be ignorant or not to know what death is like (I Thess. 4:14-18). So often we are afraid of the things that we don't understand, and when we know ahead of time just what is going to happen we aren't afraid. When we go to the doctor's office, we like to know ahead of time if it is going to hurt. Our minds are greatly relieved if we are sure we don't have to have any shots. God wants us to know ahead of time

just what death and what the life after death
are like. So His Word has told us just what to
expect. He said that our souls and spirits go
straight to Heaven to be with the Lord. They
can never die. Our bodies will be put into a
grave to wait until Christ comes again for the
resurrection. Christ will appear in the air with
all those Christians who have died. They will
receive their bodies made anew and will be re-
united to their souls and spirits. All the living
Christians will be given their new bodies without dying. All of us will meet the Lord in the
air and go together to live with Him forever.

Easter should be a time of real rejoicing for
us if we are Christians, because all of these
things are possible for us only because Christ
died on the cross for us and rose again (I Cor.
15:3, 4). Knowing these things should take
away the fear of dying.

If you have never been saved, Easter will be
a day of solemn warning to you that you cannot
have a part in this wonderful resurrection when
Christ comes again. You will be resurrected at
another time and be judged, because you re-
fused to take Christ as your Saviour, and then
you will be sent away into everlasting punishment. Right now, ask Christ to come into your
heart. He is more anxious to save you than you

are to receive Him. Just say in your heart, "Dear Jesus, please save me. Amen." Then you will be saved and have a part in this first resurrection (John 11:25, 26).

A NEW HOUSE

PREPARATION: Find some nails, small pieces of lumber, etc., from a house that is being torn down.

PRESENTATION

The other day, I was passing an old house that is being torn down and I picked up some nails and other things that are being discarded. Here are some nails that have held that house together for nearly a hundred years. This is a piece of molding that must have been beautiful before the paint began to peel. There are some people who remember that house when it was still new, and some can even remember being entertained in the house. They don't like to see it torn down. But the way it was, it couldn't be used by anyone. The roof is coming off, the porch floor is completely gone, the windows have all been broken. The plumbing isn't any good, and the foundation has almost rotted away so the house would soon fall down completely. I understand that the new owner is going to build another more beautiful house

than the one that is being taken down. It will
have a good foundation; it will have good
plumbing; and everything in this house will be
new and beautiful.

On this Easter day, we want to talk about a
new house that God has promised will be ours
because the Lord Jesus Christ died on the cross
for us and rose again on the third day (I Cor.
15:3, 4). We are promised that when this body
of ours gives out, God has prepared a new body
for us which is far better than the one we have
now. Someday we will all get old like this
house. Our bodies will have many aches and
pains, and it will be hard for us to walk and to
see, and one day our bodies will die. It shouldn't
be a time of sorrow and crying for us, or our
loved ones, because we will go to be with the
Lord. Only our bodies die, but the soul and
spirit will go immediately to be with the Lord.

Christ has gone ahead of us and He has promised that He will prepare dwelling places for
us. Then He also promised that one day He will
come again (I Thess. 4:14-18). He will appear
in the clouds, and He will bring with Him all
the Christians who have died and gone to Heav-
en. As soon as Christ comes back, the Christians who have died, and the Christians who
are still living on the earth, will all be given new

and glorious bodies. This new body will never have any pain again, and it can never die again, and it will have power to do things it has never been able to do before. The people who are lame, or blind, or paralyzed, etc., will now have wonderful, new straight bodies that will be fitted for living in Heaven. God says that "flesh and blood cannot inherit the kingdom of God," so this corrupt, earthly body must be changed before it can be ready for life in Heaven.

Instead of being afraid of dying, or sad when some Christian we loved dies, we should be very thankful because we know that being with the Lord is far better than living down here on this earth where there is so much trouble, sorrow, pain and tears, and then finally death (Rev. 21:4).

These wonderful promises of resurrection— a new body, and a new home in Heaven—are given only to those who have taken the Lord Jesus Christ as their Saviour. If you have never asked Christ to save you, I pray that you will do it right now as we are talking about the resurrection of Christ. It was because of His resurrection that we can have the blessed assurance that we will be resurrected and given new bodies to live in Heaven forever.

THANKSGIVING LESSONS

ANOTHER THANKSGIVING

PREPARATION : Secure a choir robe to take with you.

PRESENTATION

When we think about Thanksgiving, we usually think about the day that our nation has set aside as a special day of thanks for all the material blessings God has sent us. We remember this day because it was started by the Pilgrims, who came to the United States to find the freedom to worship God as they felt was right. Usually, Thanksgiving makes us think of a big turkey dinner, pie, etc., and lots of people think of Thanksgiving as a day of football games and a holiday from work.

I have brought a choir robe with me this morning because I want to talk about choirs. Have you heard a big, big choir sing in church? When we hear the blend of several hundred voices, it just seems to lift us up and make us sit on the edge of the seat. Sometimes, when I have heard some wonderful choir music, full of praises to God, I wonder if the singing in

Heaven is going to sound something like that.

There is a day of thanksgiving still to come for all Christians. That thanksgiving is going to be in Heaven, and isn't just for one day. It is going to last throughout all eternity. All the angels and other heavenly hosts, and all Christians who will be in Heaven then, are going to join together in one great choir to give praise and thanksgiving to the Lord Jesus Christ. Our praise and thanksgiving will be to Him because of His death on the cross to save us from our sins. We are going to sing a "new song" about the death and the resurrection of the Lord Jesus Christ for all the people of the world. (Read Rev. 5:9-12.) Can you imagine what it will be like to have a choir of ten thousand times ten thousand, and thousands of thousands? That is too much for us to number. We are also told that this choir will be made up of people from every tribe, tongue, and nation of the world. (Also see Rev. 7:9.)

We are going to wear robes to sing in this heavenly choir too. Most of our churches have choir robes for the singers in their choirs. In Heaven everyone must have a robe to be there and to sing in this choir. Our robes are going to be the white robe of righteousness that the Lord Jesus Christ has given to all who have asked Him to come into their hearts. When Christ saves us He washes our sins away, and in their place He gives us His righteousness (II Cor. 5:21). Now when God looks at us, He sees us through Christ's righteousness. (Also see Rev. 7:14.)

If praise and thanksgiving are so important to God that we are going to spend all eternity singing praises to the Lord Jesus Christ for what He has done, don't you think it is very important that we start spending much time in thanksgiving and praise right here and now? Thanksgiving shouldn't be confined mostly to one day or one season of the year. It should be an attitude of our hearts all through everyday. If you don't think that you have been thankful enough for what God has done for you, just ask Him to help you to have a grateful heart. Think over all the blessings you have and thank God for each one of them. If you keep your heart free of sin, the Holy Spirit will do a special work of putting praise and thanksgiving to the Lord in your heart.

THANK YOU

PREPARATION: Buy something that will be suitable for a boy or girl, and wrap it as a gift. A thank-you note will do as a substitute.

PRESENTATION

When I talk about Thanksgiving Day, what is the first thing that comes to your minds? If you are real honest, I think you would say a big turkey dinner, or a holiday from school, or a football game. God's Word has much to say about our giving thanks for the things that He has given us. He intends for us to give Him thanks all the time every day (Ps. 95:2), and not just one day in the year.

I have brought a gift for one of you in this class. Who would like to have it? You may come up here and get it. (Open gift.) When you took the gift, you said, "Thank you." Why did you say that? Yes, it is a way of showing me that you appreciate the fact that I brought you a gift. When we get gifts from one another we are very careful to express our thanks. I have a letter here thanking me for a wedding present that I sent to a couple I know. They wanted me to know that they appreciated the gift I sent to them.

Is this the only gift you received today? It is? It isn't your birthday or Christmas, so you don't think that you should be getting gifts. Did you have breakfast this morning? Well, wasn't that food a gift? God gave your father the ability to make the money necessary to buy the food for your mother to make your breakfast. Did you thank God for that food? The Lord Jesus Christ never ate a meal without first giving thanks for the food that His heavenly Father had provided. Jim, I see that you have some nice clothes on this morning. Did you give thanks to God for providing those clothes for you? Do you know that there are many boys and girls in the world who do not have enough clothes to keep them warm? Then shouldn't we be very careful to give God thanks for our clothes? You have a lovely home, Jim. I saw it this morning as I drove by. Have you thanked God for that home? Many do not have any homes. All of you boys and girls have parents, but there are thousands of boys and girls who have lost their parents. Jim, are you happy to live in the United States where we have freedom to go to church, to read our Bibles, to go

to school, and to be safe from harm? Have you
thanked God for that? Someday, God might
take away our freedom to make us appreciate
it enough to continually thank Him for it. All
of you boys and girls have health and strength,
or you wouldn't be here today. Have you
thanked God for these things? Many boys and
girls are lame and blind and some have to stay
in bed all the time.

Suppose God would suddenly take away all
the gifts that He has given us, only then would
we realize just how much He has done for us.
Everything that we have belongs to God and is
given to us by God. We are so careful to thank
people for their gifts, so please be very careful
to thank God for His gifts. Jim, if I brought
you a gift every time we had a class meeting
and you never said "Thank you" to me, do you
think I would keep on bringing gifts for you?
You are right, I am sure I wouldn't. But many
expect God to keep on giving them gifts. It is
so easy to say thanks when we truly appreciate
what has been done for us. If we just keep
thinking about all the things that God has done
for us, we can't help but give Him thanks constantly.

Most of all, we should give thanks for the
death of the Lord Jesus Christ for our sins, and

that we can take Him as our Saviour (II Cor.
9:15). We should be thankful that God has
taken us as His dear children in a special way
since we have let the Lord Jesus Christ come
into our hearts. We should be thankful for the
Bible that tells us all our wonderful spiritual
blessings. We should be thankful for the right
we have to come to God in prayer to ask Him
for the things that we want and need. Let's all
be determined not to take God's wonderful gifts
for granted. Let's give thanks for everything
all the time.

PRAISE AND THANKSGIVING

PREPARATION: Make four cards about three by ten inches. Print THANKSGIVING on the first; print THANKS FOR GOD'S GIFTS on the second, and tie the two together. Print PRAISE on the third, and THANKS FOR GOD HIMSELF on the fourth, and tie these two together. Hold the second card behind the first, and the fourth card behind the third, until they are lowered during the lesson.

PRESENTATION

Many boys and girls think that the first Thanksgiving Day ever celebrated was when the Pilgrims were first settling in our country and entertained the Indians at a feast. But God told the children of Israel to set aside a week for giving thanks. We are told about it way back in the first part of our Bibles (Lev. 23:33-44). This was a feast to God for the wonderful harvest of food that He gave them. It was something like our Thanksgiving. These people had many sacrifices of animals to make, but we don't have to do that since the Lord Jesus Christ died on the cross for our sins (Heb. 9:12, 13; 10:11, 12). Now, all we have to do is to take Christ as our Saviour and He will wash away our sins.

God has asked us as Christians to make different kinds of sacrifices for Him. One of these is to offer a sacrifice of thanksgiving and praise. In this Thanksgiving week, we want to talk about thanksgiving and praise.

(Show card with THANKSGIVING.) We shouldn't have to be told to give thanks to God for all His blessings, but over and over in the Bible we are told to give thanks. (Read Eph. 5:20.) God knows our hearts (Jer. 17:9), and He knows we need to be constantly reminded that everything we have comes from Him. We get so used to our blessings we often forget that God is the One who is providing for all our needs. There is a long list of terrible sins in the first chapter of Romans, and one of the first sins was that of being unthankful. Being unthankful hurts our heavenly Father and often leads to other sins. What does thanksgiving mean? (Let the other card down.) Thanksgiving means "giving thanks for God's gifts." We could stay here for days naming the things that God has given us and giving Him thanks for them, and still forget a lot of them. We ought to get in the habit of thinking of all the things God has given us, and thanking Him as they come to our minds. We should thank Him for even the little things in our lives because nothing is too little for Him to give us. We should be thankful for the unpleasant things, because He has promised that everything He sends into our lives is just what we need to make us more like Christ. By reading the Bible and talking to Him in prayer, we will learn more of what He has done for us and so find ourselves giving more thanks to Him.

(Show card with PRAISE.) Usually, people use the term thanksgiving and praise together because they think they mean the same thing. We find in God's Word that they are different, and also that God expects both from His children. (Let down the lower part of the card.) Praise is appreciation for God Himself. It is being thankful that we know the only living and true God, and being occupied with God Himself rather than with the gifts He gives us. It means wanting to talk to Him and think about Him instead of constantly asking Him for things. "Whoso offereth praise glorifieth me" (Ps. 50:23). I would be so unhappy if my daughters only spoke to me when they wanted to ask for something, and if every time I gave them a gift they just grabbed it and ran away. But that is the way we often treat God. Just as I want my girls to love me and want to be with me even when I don't have any gifts for them, so God wants us to love Him apart from His giving things to us. Let's offer real praise this Thanksgiving, as well as giving thanks for God's gifts.

THANKSGIVING IN PRAYER

PREPARATION: Make three large cardboard circles. Print WORRY on one side of the first, and NOTHING on the other side. Print PRAY on one side of the second, and EVERYTHING on the other side. Print THANKFUL on one side of the third, and ANYTHING on the other side.

PRESENTATION

Our past Presidents have set aside one day every year for our nation to give thanks to God for what He has done for us. This holiday we call Thanksgiving. Sometimes, we get the idea that one day of giving thanks is all that God requires of us, but that is not true. God wants praise and thanksgiving every day of every year. Maybe it is a good thing that our nation has a day of thanksgiving because some people might never thank God unless they were reminded.

Thanksgiving is so important to God that He has made it a necessary part of our prayer. Thanksgiving and prayer are nearly always mentioned together in the Epistles. I have three circles here to help you understand that we must give God thanks to have our prayers answered and to have the wonderful peace that "passeth understanding." (Read Phil. 4:6, 7.)

(Show the first circle.) God says that we are not to WORRY. When we are worried and upset, we are not trusting God to take care of all our needs. We can't be thankful and worried at the same time. The verse says that we are to worry about NOTHING. (Turn circle around.) NOTH-ING means nothing. It includes our school work, our home life, our health, and everything that happens to us or that will happen in the future.

(Show circle with PRAY on it.) The way to keep from worrying is to pray. This is the only way that God has planned for us to talk to Him and to ask for the things that we need (James 4:2). He knows what we need before we do, but He has planned that we get those things from Him by asking for them (Matt. 6:32). Many people only pray when they are in trouble, or when they go to church, but God wants us to "pray without ceasing" (I Thess. 5:17). You probably think that you are too busy to pray that much, but you can pray while you are walking to school, while you are playing games, while you are taking exams, as well as at night.

You should want to talk to God so much that as soon as your mind is off the things that you must do, it will automatically turn to God in prayer. (Turn circle.) We are to talk to God about EVERYTHING, even the smallest detail in our lives. Isn't it wonderful to know that God is interested in hearing about everything that you are doing? He is interested in your school work, your ball games, your Scout meetings, your television programs, your Bible reading and your witnessing to others. Nothing is too small for God's interest.

(Show circle with THANKFUL.) We are to be THANKFUL in all our prayers. To be thankful means that we are happy, content and satisfied with His will for our lives. It shows that we truly trust Him to work out all our problems and troubles, as well as the things in our lives that please us. We can be thankful even when we don't know what the future holds for us, because we can trust Him to deal with us in His wisdom and love and carry out His plans for us in His power. (Turn circle over.) It is easy to be thankful for the pleasant things in our lives, but sometimes it is very hard to be thankful for anything that we don't want to happen. But God's Word says: "In everything give thanks: for this is the will of God in Christ Jesus concerning you" (I Thess. 5:18). That means to be thankful when you are sick, when you can't have the new toys you want, when you don't get the new clothes you need, or have the vacation that you planned. God has promised that "all things work together for good" to those who are His children (Rom. 8:28). Knowing that promise can assure us that there is reason to give thanks for everything in our lives.

THANKS FOR AN UNWANTED GIFT

PREPARATION : Take a gift that has been given you for which you have no use.

PRESENTATION

I have a gift in this box. I want you to see it so I brought it with me this morning. I have been hinting and suggesting for some things that I would like to have for my birthday, and I really expected to get the things that I had asked for. When I opened my present and saw this blouse, I was terribly disappointed. I just don't have anything I can wear this with, and the color isn't what I like. I have really had a hard time figuring out just how I am going to use it. It makes me unhappy every time I look at it when I think of the things that I would rather have had for my birthday.

I have made up my mind that there is only one thing for me to do. I must wear this blouse and never let the one who gave it to me know that I didn't want it. Someone who loves me and whom I love dearly gave me this gift, and I don't want to hurt her feelings. I thanked her for it. Maybe some time later, I will find a real need for this and be glad that it was given to me.

God loves us more than any earthly person can ever love us. He sends us gifts that we may not like at times, but He sends them in His love and wisdom. He knows what is best for us to have though we may not see any need for them. We should never be disappointed with what God sends. We should always receive His gifts with thanks. In fact, God tells us in His Word that He expects us to give thanks for everything, all the time. We are not to accept it because we have to, but willingly because we love God and don't want to hurt Him. Later on, God may let us see how this has been used in our lives to make us more like Christ. If not on earth, we will certainly understand why we had so many trials when we get to Heaven.

It is easy to be thankful for all the wonderful gifts God gives us. It is pleasant to have all our prayers answered just as we ask, to have lots of friends, toys, money, loving parents, a nice home, plenty of good food and fine clothes, etc. But God requires us to give thanks for the things He sends to us that we don't want, because He has promised that "all things work together for good to them that love God, to them who are the called according to his purpose" (Rom. 8:28). We are to be thankful when our school work gets hard, and we don't like our teacher. We are asked to be thankful when someone we love dies, as hard as that may be. We should give thanks for disappointments of not receiving the gifts we want, for not having the friends we had hoped for, when we aren't chosen to be on the ball team, or when we are ill, or lose our pets. We are even to give thanks when our homes are broken up, or our parents are separated. God uses all these things to make us live closer to Him and to trust Him more.

Now, it would be very foolish to be thankful for all the unpleasant things unless God had told us to be thankful. God never asks us to do something without telling us why. God says that His way of doing things is perfect (Ps. 18:30). He says that He loves us and only sends those things that will make us more like Christ. (Read Rom. 8:28, with verse 29.) God also promises that He will never leave us nor forsake us, and He says that His grace is sufficient for every need, no matter how great. How wonderful it is to trust God so much that we can give Him thanks for everything—even the hard, unpleasant things!

CHRISTMAS LESSONS

GIFTS OF THE WISE MEN

PREPARATION: Take along some gold jewelry, some perfume, and a sticky, white substance which is perfumed (such as cold cream).

PRESENTATION

What is the first thing you think of when I mention Christmas? If you are really honest, I believe you would say that you think about receiving gifts more than anything else. Christmas is a time of giving and receiving gifts. We are not sure just where we got the idea. There were no gifts exchanged that first Christmas, but the Bible tells us that the Wise Men brought gifts to the Lord Jesus Christ (Matt. 2:11). After the Wise Men had worshiped Christ, they gave Him gifts of gold, frankincense and myrrh. These were very expensive gifts that they had brought from their home country. These gifts probably cost all the money they had.

We have no way of knowing whether the gold was in pieces or was made up in jewelry. I have some gold jewelry here this morning to remind us of this gift. Gold costs a lot of money and it takes much labor and time spent in work to buy it. Maybe the gold will give us some idea of what gift we might give to the Lord Jesus Christ. God has saved us through the work of the Lord Jesus Christ that we might serve Him. (Read Eph. 2:8-10.) God planned, even before He saved us, the things that He wants us to do for Him. You see we don't work for our salvation but because of it. (Also see I Cor. 3:12-15.) We are to do what God wants us to do. He says He will show us His will if we honestly want to do it (John 7:17).

Frankincense was another gift that the Wise Men brought to Christ. I have a bottle of perfume here to make us think of this gift, for this is what frankincense is. It smells sweet. It was used in the Old Testament as incense for worship in the Tabernacle. When the priests went into the Tabernacle to minister, this perfume clung to their clothes and as they returned to the people everyone knew that they had been in the presence of the Lord (Exod. 30-34-38).

In the New Testament, we are told by Paul that we are to be an odor, or a sweet fragrance unto the Lord, by our witness and testimony. The way we live as Christians is so important because others are watching. If our lives are full of sin, they will not want to know Christ.

But if we are sweet, kind, loving persons, they will want to take Christ as their Saviour too. The only way we can live a life that is pleasing to God, and a witness to others, is by the help of the Holy Spirit. We are given a list of the things that the Spirit will produce in us if we will let Him (Gal. 5:22, 23).

The third gift that the Wise Men brought to Christ was myrrh.

This was a sticky type of perfume, but it was used mostly to anoint the dead (John 19:39). Nicodemus brought myrrh and aloes to wrap in the linen which they put on the body of the Lord Jesus Christ.

Christ gave His life that you and I might escape spiritual death. The Bible tells us that we are to die to self, and to all selfish desires. We are to remember that we have been crucified with Christ (Gal. 2:20). Now we should walk in "newness of life," and our lives should be completely controlled by Him. Last of all, we are to present our bodies as living sacrifices to God. Only as we do this can we carry out the good and acceptable will of God.

Did you ever wish that you could give a big, big gift to the Lord Jesus Christ to show Him how much you appreciate what He has done for you? Would you like to give Him a million dollars? The best gift you can give Him is your-self. He wants you more than He wants your money. He wants you to take Him as your Saviour first, then give Him your life in service and witness.

CHRISTMAS LIGHTS

PREPARATION: Secure an extension cord, a light
bulb of any size, and a circuit breaker. Find
a place to connect it to an outlet.

PRESENTATION

At Christmas time, we see more lights than
at any other time of the year. There are long
strings of lights over the streets, on trees,
around people's houses, and inside stores. There
are so many lights of different colors and kinds
at Christmas that sometimes it is hard to tell
the difference between them and the traffic
lights and the store signs. I have brought an
electric light with me this morning because I
want to talk about lights.

Lights are so important. We need lights in
hospitals, in restaurants and in churches, as
well as in our homes. We need them to see to
sew, to eat, to play, and to read. Sometimes a
storm breaks the connection in our houses and
our lights go out. The clocks stop running, the
refrigerator begins to defrost, and the TV won't

work. It is hard on everyone when the power fails.

This electric cord has been plugged in the wall outlet, and a bulb put on this end, so the light will shine. This is to represent a Christian boy or girl, because the light in the bulb makes us think of the Lord Jesus Christ who said that He is the Light of the world. Christ said that we are to shine as lights for Him in this world. It is God's plan that each Christian should show forth the Lord Jesus Christ. He could have planned other ways to have people hear about salvation but He didn't. His only plan is to have us tell others how to be saved. We must realize how important it is for us to let our lights shine for Him.

(Slip a circuit breaker in the end of the cord.) Now watch the light. What happened? The light went off. Oh, now it's on again! It is hard on our eyes to watch it blink off and on. If you tried to read by such a light it would be worse than no light at all, because when the light goes out it leaves a bright spot before your eyes. Then when it's on again, your eyes can't adjust fast enough to the brightness of the light.

Some Christian boys and girls are just like this light. One day they are shining brightly for the Lord Jesus Christ, and the next day they are cross, mean and disobedient. One minute they are telling how much they love the Lord Jesus Christ, and the next minute they are sinning by doing some things that the unsaved children do. They don't mind doing the things that will show themselves off and let others see how important they are, but they never want to do the little jobs that really help but don't give them any special credit. This light doesn't do anyone any good as it goes off and on. It just draws attention to itself. Even though it bothers your eyes, you can't help but watch it blink. When we are merely drawing attention to ourselves, our shining for the Lord Jesus Christ will never make someone else interested in taking Him as their Saviour. This light also reminds me of the boys and girls who promise to help their Sunday school teacher, or to attend church, or to speak at one of their meetings, but if they find something else they would rather do they don't show up. Boys and girls like this don't care about their testimony or about winning others to Christ.

When you are riding along in your car and see the Christmas lights blinking off and on, I hope that you will remember this lesson. Tell

God right now that you are determined with His help to be the steady, bright light that shines all the time, every place you are, for His glory, and to win others to Christ.

HEART OF JOY

PREPARATION: Make two large cardboard hearts
—one with uneven lines on it to look like it
has been broken, and the other with a picture
of Christ in the center, surrounded by mu-
sical notes.

PRESENTATION

Mary and Joseph were engaged and making
plans for their wedding. They were very happy
that at last they would be together in their own
home. But before they were married, an angel
came to Mary and told her that God had other
plans for her life. She had pleased God, and He
had chosen her to be the mother of the Lord
Jesus Christ. She couldn't understand how God
was going to work all this out, but she was willing to do what God wanted her to. No matter
what it would cost her, Mary planned to do
God's will. (Read Luke 1:38.)

It wasn't long before Mary found out that
doing God's will wasn't easy. It was very hard.
She had a broken heart. (Show broken heart.)
People thought that she was a sinful woman

and talked about her. Her family and friends, and Joseph, the man who loved her, thought that she had sinned. Mary went to visit her cousin Elisabeth. Joseph wanted to break their engagement. But God was taking care of Mary, and later He sent an angel to tell Joseph that Mary was doing God's will, and told him to take care of her and the Baby Jesus. We know that Joseph did what he was told.

Some people think that as soon as we take the Lord Jesus Christ as our Saviour, everything in our lives will be rosy and wonderful. Many think that as long as we are doing God's will, we will have everything the way we want it. But that is not always true. Sometimes it is God's will for us to lose a loved one, to be very ill, to suffer because we don't have enough money, and many other ways. God knows in His wisdom and love what is necessary for us to bear that we might learn the lesson He wants to teach us. It is very important that we find out God's will and be willing to do it (John 7:17). When we are willing, He will show us what He wants us to do. Then no matter how hard it is to do, God will be with us and see us through all our trials.

Even though all the things that happened to Mary would cause her a broken heart, we find that she had a heart full of joy in the Lord. (Show other heart.) While Mary was visiting with Elisabeth, she sang a wonderful song that is often called the "Magnificat." It is Mary's song of testimony and praise and joy in the Lord and in having a part in giving a Saviour to the world. (Read Luke 1:46-49.) Isn't that beautiful? Can't you imagine how radiant Mary's face was when she spoke those words? Mary was happy because she was doing God's will. The happiness was the kind that only the Lord gives and does not come from our natural circumstances. Mary was also happy because God was using her to be the one through whom the Saviour of the world was to be born. He was Mary's Saviour too, though she was to be His mother. Mary was rewarded in a special way for doing God's will. As long as the world shall stand, Mary will be remembered and honored for what she did. As long as we have a Bible, people will read about Mary and how God used her.

The Bible tells us in many verses that all Christians have to suffer trials, chastisements, and testings of various kinds (Heb. 12:6). It is hard for us to find any happiness in these things, but God says that we can find real joy and peace in Him even while we are going through trials. He has promised to always be with us and never forsake us. He has also promised that His grace is sufficient for every need we have (II Cor. 12:9). If you are having any troubles in your life now, remember how Mary was tried even while she was doing God's will. And remember, too, that nothing can come into your life that God doesn't allow and He will give you the strength for every need.

GIFTS OF THE SPIRIT

PREPARATION: Get five boxes of different sizes so they can be put one into the other. Put one of the illustrations suggested in the lesson in each box. Put them together and wrap the outside box like a Christmas present. Carefully read I Corinthians 12 and Ephesians 4.

PRESENTATION

We have all heard people give thanks for the gifts that God gives us. In fact, our country has set aside one day each year for special thanksgiving for what God has done for us. At Christmas time, we heard a lot of people talk about the gifts that we have because of Christ's birth, death and resurrection. There are many spiritual gifts we enjoy because we have taken Christ as our Saviour. Have you ever heard anyone give a prayer of thanks for the gifts of the Holy Spirit? Until a few years ago, I never knew that the Holy Spirit gave Christians special gifts. Maybe you haven't heard about it either.

I have brought a Christmas box with me this

morning to show you some of the gifts that the
Spirit gives to Christians. Before we open this
gift, I want to read a verse from I Corinthians
12:7. If we had time to read the verses before
this one, we would see that the Holy Spirit has
given every Christian a gift. Some may have
only one gift, and some may have more than
one. This gift (or gifts) is to be used for the
Lord and not for ourselves. Have you heard
some people say that they can't do anything for
the Lord because they don't have any special
gift, or talent? They look at other folks and
think that others have gifts and they don't.
But we know from God's Word that all Christians are given at least one gift to be used in
God's service.

Back in the days when our Bibles were first
written, the Holy Spirit gave some people the
ability to prophesy, or tell what will happen in
the future. There were gifts of apostles, or the
men who knew the Lord Jesus Christ and wit-
nessed to Him at that time. There were also
some gifts given to men in Bible times to heal
and to talk in tongues.

We want to open our Christmas gift now and
talk about the gifts that the Spirit gives to each
Christian in this day. (Open the first box and
show a small Bible.) One gift of the Spirit is

the gift of teaching God's Word. There **are** some people who have a special ability to make the truths in the Bible plain to others. They can't do this themselves but only as the Spirit gives them the gift to do it. (Open the next box and show a picture of a shepherd.) Another gift the Spirit gives is the ability to be a good pastor. There are men who are chosen by the Spirit to preach the Word in the church, and to help the members whenever they are in trouble or sorrow, or need advice. (Open the next box and show a picture of Christ.) There are other people who are given special ability to be evangelists. These are used in a special way to preach the Gospel and to tell others how to be saved. We can all probably name some well-known evangelists, and hundreds of people are saved every time they preach. (Open the next box and show a picture of a church.) The next gift of the Spirit is the gift of governments. That means that there are people who have the gift of being good officers in the church. They are given the ability to be good leaders in God's work. (Open the next box and show as many illustrations as possible of the things mentioned in the following.) Every one can easily have this gift. It is the gift of helps. That means the ability to do the manual labor necessary to carry on the work of the church, or to help other Christians or the unsaved. Good mothers who take care of their families, nurses who care for the sick, those who help keep the church clean, those who entertain, those who spend time in real, earnest prayer, and those who give money for the work of the Lord, either at home or on the mission fields, are the ones who have the gifts of helping.

All of us are given at least one of these gifts, or we will as we get older. It is important that we find out what gift the Spirit has given us and exercise it, or use it. Don't waste time wishing that you had a gift you see in someone else. God requires you to use the ability He has given you according to His will, and He rewards us according to how we use it. Every gift is equally important to the work of Christ, and whatever gift the Spirit has given you is just as important to you as the ones He has given to others. Just thank Him for what He has seen fit to give you and use it to His glory (I Cor. 12:28).

GIVING

PREPARATION : Wrap and take the gifts that you usually give your class at Christmas time. If you can't do that, take a few wrapped Christmas gifts.

PRESENTATION

Here on the table I have some Christmas gifts that I am giving to all of you this year. But before I give them to you, I am going to use them as an object to teach us a lesson about giving.

Every Christmas I have a wonderful time planning, shopping, and wrapping gifts for the people I love. Sometimes it means I have to go without something to buy all the presents. But it means more to me to give gifts to others than to get gifts for myself.

At Christmas time, God gave the greatest gift of all—His own precious Son. Do you know why God gave the Lord Jesus Christ to a world of sinners who had no use for Him? A very familiar verse tells us the reason. Let's repeat John 3:16 together. It was because of

His wonderful love for us that He was willing and happy to send His Son down here on earth so that He could be the Saviour of mankind. At Christmas time, the Lord Jesus Christ also gave a wonderful gift to us. He gave Himself and His life for our sins. (Read II Cor. 8:9.) The Lord Jesus Christ gave up His wonderful throne in Heaven, where He was with His Father and was surrounded by the praise and worship and obedience of the angels and other heavenly hosts. He came to the poorest kind of parents, was born in a stable and put in a manger. When He was thirty-three years old, He went to the cross to die for the sins of the world. He did it because He loves us, and He was willing to die for us because He knew that it was the only way that we could be saved (Heb. 12:2).

When we think of giving to the Lord at other times as well as at Christmas, we have the example of the sacrifice that God and the Lord Jesus Christ made for us. When we think of what they did for us, how can we do less than to sacrifice some of the things that we want to give to the Lord's work? God doesn't want what we have left over and what we can easily spare. He wants us to love Him so much that we will give Him the best that we have.

Paul gives definite instructions to all Christians of how we are to give to the Lord's work in II Corinthians 9. First, we are to give according to the amount that God has seen fit to give us. The person who makes a lot of money should give much, and the one who makes only a little will give less. Second, we are to give according to what God wants us to give and not because someone says that we must give a certain amount. Third, we are to give cheerfully for God wants us to be happy about what we are giving to Him. If one of my daughters came to me with a gift and said that her daddy had insisted that she give me a gift, but she didn't want to spend her money that way, do you think I would want that gift? Of course not. It would make me very sad to know that my daughter didn't love me enough to give me a gift because she wanted to and not because she was forced to give it. Fourth, we are to give because our gifts bring thanksgiving to God. When someone is saved, he thanks God for the money that was used to bring him to Christ. When we help a missionary, he thanks God for that help. When those in financial need have help, they thank God for food and clothes. Last, we are to give every week (I Cor. 16:2). Every Sunday, we are to plan to give to the

Lord's work in proportion to the amount that the Lord has given us through the week.

All of these instructions on giving are for Christians. No amount of money will buy salvation for you. God is first interested in having you take the Lord Jesus Christ as your Saviour, and then He will be happy to have your gifts for His work. God wants you to give Him yourself first, and then He will tell you what He wants you to do in appreciation and love.

MISSIONARY LESSONS

1. Idols
2. Sickness
3. Map of the World
4. It Pays to Advertise
5. Stop and Go

IDOLS

PREPARATION: If possible, make a small snow man and freeze until ready for use. If this is impossible, use a picture of a snow man.

PRESENTATION

Most of you boys and girls have seen a snow man even in our most southern states. Almost the first thing you want to do when you go out to play in the snow is to make a snow man. Even grown men and women like to make snow men, and I have seen them work for hours to make a perfect-looking creation. After they get the body formed, they usually put a cane in its hand, a hat on its head, and a scarf around its neck. Then they carefully make the eyes, nose and mouth with small stones, or buttons, or pieces of coal. But no matter how long they work or how perfect it is, it is still just snow! The eyes can't see, the nose can't smell, the ears can't hear, and the mouth can't speak. The legs can't walk, the arms can't move, and of course, it can't think because it has no brains. When the weather warms up a bit and the sun comes

113

out, what happens? It gradually melts and is soon gone.

You and I know better than to worship a snow man. We know it can't be God. First, it can't be God because we made it ourselves. Second, it can't be God because it has no ability to think or act; and third, because we know that it can't last very long. All of us have heard about the only living and true God who is our heavenly Father.

There are millions of people in this world who worship idols very much like this snow man. Everyone feels a need to worship something, and since they don't know the true God, they make idols to worship. Some idols are made of gold, of silver, of stone, and of paper. Let me read you some verses from Psalm 115:4-8, in which God is describing an idol. Do you notice how much an idol is like this snow man? They are made by men themselves; they can't see, hear, smell or walk, etc.

It seems strange to us that these people think that idols can help them, but their lives are so full of fear and superstition that they don't know any better. They don't have churches, preachers, the Bible, and Christian literature. Most of them can't read, so even if they had a Bible it wouldn't do them any good. Someone has to go to these foreign lands to tell them about the Lord Jesus Christ, and about God our heavenly Father. They have to be told how they can be saved. Someone has to translate the Bible into their language, and then teach them how to read, and how to understand God's message from the Word.

God needs you to go any place where He may want to send you to give the Gospel message to people who have never heard. Is there anyone here who feels that God has shown you that He wants you to be a missionary? I know some boys and girls your age who already feel that God has called them to be missionaries and ministers. The important thing for you to do right now is to be willing to do whatever God tells you is His will. Can you honestly say, "Lord, I am willing to do Your will"?

SICKNESS

PREPARATION: Secure as large a cardboard pill box as possible from the drugstore. On the top, print FOR CURE OF SIN-SICK PEOPLE on the first line. On the second, print TO BE TAKEN INTO THE HEART ONLY ONCE. Put a picture of Christ inside of the pill box. Also take a bottle of Alka-Seltzer or aspirin.

PRESENTATION

I have brought a bottle of Alka-Seltzer with me this morning and a cardboard pill box like we sometimes get from the drugstore. Each bottle of medicine tells us what it is to be taken for and gives definite instructions for the amount we are to use. (Read some of the instructions on the bottle.) Most of us don't like to take medicine but there are times when we need it. We should be very thankful that we have medicine, doctors, nurses and hospitals to take care of us when we are sick. Even when people take a lot of medicine, have good doctors to care for them, and operations, some of them

116

die. We know that all of us will have to die some day.

God's Word says that there is something very wrong with everyone who is born into this world. We are not physically sick, but we are spiritually dead. (Rom. 3:10; and Rom. 3:23.) People in England, Africa, China, Russia, Mexico, and in the United States have all sinned. Sin separates us from God. "There is none righteous, no, not one." The world is spiritually sick because of sin. (Repeat Rom. 6:23.) The result of sin is always spiritual death. This doesn't mean having our bodies die, but means that we are separated from God's presence. No matter what we try to do to pay for our sins, like joining the church, giving money, and being the best we can, we can't pay for our sins. God loves us so much that He doesn't want us to die for our sins. He planned a different way for us.

This other pill box I have will show us the answer to what we can do about our sins to escape spiritual death. The label on the top of this box gives us the directions for taking this medicine, and tells how it should be used. Listen while I read what is says, FOR CURE OF SIN-SICK PEOPLE. Here are the instructions for taking this medicine. (Read TO BE TAKEN INTO

THE HEART ONLY ONCE.) My, that does sound
like powerful medicine! It seems different from
the usual kind of medicine, doesn't it? (Open
the box and show the picture of Christ.) We
must take the Lord Jesus Christ as our Saviour.
All we have to do is to ask Him to come into our
hearts once and He will always stay there. He
will forgive our sins and give us His righteousness in their place. Now we know that we shall
never be separated from God and that we will
live through all eternity in Heaven.

You and I have often heard the story of how
to take Christ as Saviour, but there are many
boys and girls and grown-up people who have
never heard that Christ died for them. It isn't
fair that they should die because they have
never heard when we know the truth. Some
people who know Christ as Saviour must go to
these countries to tell others about Christ too.

If you were a doctor and had the right kind
of medicine to make all the sick people in the
world well again, I am sure that you would go
quickly to help these people. You are a spiritual
doctor when you know Christ as Saviour, and
you know the cure for sin. You have the answer
to the needs of these sin-sick people of the
world, and you should be just as anxious to
make them spiritually alive as to cure their

sick bodies. God may call some of you to be missionaries. I hope that He will and that you will gladly go to tell others about the Lord Jesus Christ.

MAP OF THE WORLD

PREPARATION: Take with you a map of the world or a globe.

PRESENTATION

I have brought a map of the world with me today because it reminds me of a wonderful verse that God has given in His Word.

When we take the Lord Jesus Christ as our Saviour, something happens to our sins. Listen to a precious promise God has made. (Read Psalm 103:12.) "Transgressions" means the same thing as sins. God says that our sins are taken away as far as the east is from the west. How far is the east from the west? How far have our sins been removed? If we started in (name your town and state) and traveled and traveled until we reached China (point to China on the map), would that be how far our sins have been removed? No! In China the east is on beyond us like the horizon. The same is true about the west. The east and the west never come together, no matter where we are or how far we travel. We may go round and round the

120

world, but there will always be an east on one
side and a west on the other. This is God's way
of showing that our sins have been removed so
far from us that they can never be found again.
In another verse, God says that our sins have
been cast into the deepest sea. No one knows
just how deep the sea is. Another verse says
that God has put our sins behind His back. He
can never see them again when they are behind
Him (Isa. 38:17.) So God is telling us that our
sins are lost and gone forever.

Have you ever wondered how God can remove
our sins? All of our sins were put on the Lord
Jesus Christ while He hung on the cross, and
His death paid the price that God required for
our sins. Now, when we ask the Lord Jesus
Christ to come into our hearts to save us, God
can remove all of our sins so that they can never
be found again. This is the only way our sins
can be forgiven. You cannot pay to have your
sins removed. Joining the church or being bap-
tized doesn't affect your sins. God has promised
that when we take Christ as our Saviour, He
will remove our sins "as far as the east is from
the west."

This is the most wonderful promise that a
person can ever know. Let's look at the map
of the world again. Do you realize that there

are millions of people around this world who
have never heard this promise? (Point to special places that the children have studied about
where missionary work is being carried on, and
where there is need for more missionary work.)

Oftentimes we show by our thoughts and
actions that we think Christ died only for us, or
that we don't really care about these millions
of other people who have never had a chance
to hear about what the Lord Jesus Christ has
done for them. God loves them as much as He
does us, and He wants them to hear the story
of salvation just as much. Lots of boys and
girls want to plan their own lives. They want
to stay here at home where they can have all
the latest conveniences and where they think
they can make a lot of money. Take another
look at the map. Can you really plan to stay
at home knowing about these people who have
no one to tell them about the Lord Jesus Christ?
You are responsible before God to go if He is
calling you to the mission field. Listen to what
God has planned for you and tell Him that you
are willing to do what He wants you to do.

IT PAYS TO ADVERTISE

PREPARATION: Take a magazine with colored advertisements in it.

PRESENTATION

There is an old saying, "It pays to advertise." We know that is true because many millions of dollars are spent every year advertising products in magazines, in newspapers, over the radio and television. I brought a magazine this morning that is full of nice looking advertisements. Look at some of these. (Turn to some of the pages that show colored advertisements.) Here is a beautiful car. Anyone who sees this picture will want one. Here is a lovely stove in such attractive surroundings that I am sure every woman who sees it will want a stove like this for her kitchen. Here are some nice toys and games that I am sure you boys and girls will want. Many different companies make many different kinds of products, and they want to sell them, so they put attractive ads in the magazines to make us want to buy their products. They put good-looking people in their pictures, and many times pictures of well-known people to make us believe that what they have to sell is the very best on the market. These men go to all this work and expense because they want to make money.

God has saved us and left us in this world to be an advertisement for the Lord Jesus Christ. We are to tell others about Christ because we love Him and want to make Him attractive to others so they will want to be saved too (II Cor. 5:14). There are many things that we will do for love that we won't do for money. It is much easier to work for love, and we do a better job for love's sake. Love should always be our motive for what we do for God. However, God has also promised to reward us for what we do for Him.

God has only one plan for getting the message of salvation to the people of the world. That plan is to have the Christians tell others how to be saved. God could have sent millions of angels to tell people how to be saved, but He didn't. He could have spoken from Heaven so that all the people of the world could hear Him, but that was not His plan. He could have written the message of salvation across the sky so everyone could read it, but that wasn't His plan.

God's plan is for those of us who have taken

the Lord Jesus Christ as Saviour to tell others how He died on the cross for them too. He has a plan for your lives. He may not have told you yet what He plans for you to do, but He will in plenty of time. He may send you to the jungles, to South America, to Mexico, to Europe, and maybe even to Russia. He may plan for you to live right at home and give the message of salvation to your friends and neighbors.

While you are waiting for God to tell you what He wants you to do with your life, it is important to be missionaries right here at home. You can tell others how to be saved in your school, in your home, among your playmates, and your neighbors. When Christ was here on earth, He said that we are responsible to tell the good news of salvation to all the world and that means right here at home too. If you aren't faithfully giving out the good news now, how can God trust you to give it out on the mission field later on? Now is the time to get ready for what the Lord will call you to do later.

STOP AND GO

PREPARATION: Make a construction-paper traffic sign with STOP and GO in the usual red and green colors.

PRESENTATION

Here is a paper traffic signal that I made for our object lesson this morning. You have all watched the lights turn from one color to another. Everyone understands that we are to *stop* when the light is red and *go* when the light is green.

There are times when God wants us to stop and there are times when God wants us to go. The angel who appeared to the women at Christ's tomb on Easter morning might give us a good idea of what God wants us to do.

When the women came to the tomb, they looked inside and found that the body of the Lord Jesus Christ was gone. An angel spoke to them. The angel said, "He is not here: for he is risen, as he said. Come, see the place where the Lord lay. And go quickly, and tell his disciples that he is risen from the dead"

(Matt. 28:6, 7a). They had to stop for proof that He was truly the Son of God because of His resurrection, and then they were told to go out and tell others so they could believe in Christ too.

That is God's plan for each one of us. We must first STOP to take Christ as our own Saviour. We have to believe that He died on the cross to save us and was resurrected on the third day to prove that He is the very Son of God and can truly save us. Then we are responsible to GO and tell others quickly about Christ's death and resurrection.

Just before Christ went back to Heaven, He gathered His disciples around Him and told them His plan for getting the Gospel out to those who had never seen Him or heard His messages. He said that each one who knew Him was to go and tell others who had not heard. (Read Matt. 28:19, 20.)

Christ is speaking to us today as well as to the disciples, for it is still God's plan for reaching the people of the world with the message of salvation. Christ said that we are to GO. Where are we to go? You and I are not given the privilege of deciding *where* we are going to tell others about Christ. God has a will for each one of us. He knows where He wants us to be and where He can best use us. If you are willing to go wherever God wants you to, He has promised to show you His will (John 7:17). He will then show you where He wants you to go to school to be trained in the Bible and how to do missionary work. You don't need to worry about any of these things if you just take one step at a time as God shows you His will.

God wants the very best kind of young people to be missionaries. That means you must be good in your school work. You must take good care of your bodies so you will be physically fit for the hardships on the mission field. You must live very close to the Lord and learn the Word, so you will have a real message to take to the people in other lands who have never heard about the Lord Jesus Christ.